1. Materials

The world is full of many different materials. Some of them, such as gold, are **pure** materials. Some of them, such as seawater, are mixtures of pure materials.

▲ A house is made of things like bricks, mortar, wood and glass.

▲ Water pipes are made of copper. This is a single, pure material.

◄ Water can be a pure material. Tap water is not pure. It has things like **fluoride** mixed in it. Fluoride helps to stop tooth decay.

▲ The glass in a window is made from simpler materials.

▲ Iron is a single, pure material.

◄ Wood is a pure material made up of **carbon**, **hydrogen** and **oxygen**.

Q1 Make a list of five other materials used to make things in a house. Say whether you think each one is a mixture or a pure material.

Q2 Do you think soil is a mixture or a pure material? Explain your answer.

Q3 Name two pure materials that are part of seawater.

2. Elements, compounds, mixtures

Elements

If a piece of wood is heated very strongly it breaks down into a black **solid**. This black solid will not break down any more. It is called carbon and it is an **element**.

An element is a single material. It cannot be split into simpler materials.

There are 92 elements that can be found on the Earth. The photographs show some of them.

▲ Mercury ▲ Magnesium ▲ Iron ▲ Bromine ▲ Silicon

- Elements are made up of tiny pieces (**particles**) called **atoms**.
- An atom is the smallest part of an element that can exist.
- Atoms are very small. About four million hydrogen atoms would fit into this 1 mm gap. →|←
- All the atoms of an element are alike. Different elements have different atoms.

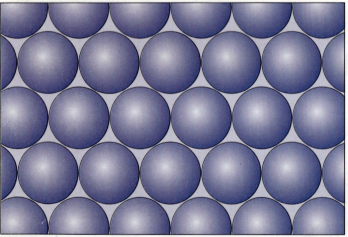 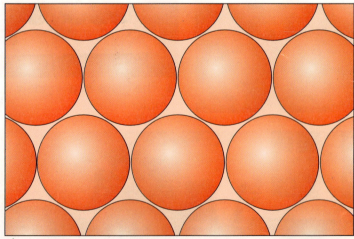

▲ Element A is made up of atoms. ▲ Element B is made up of atoms. They are different from the atoms of element A.

Q1 What is an element?

Q2 What is an atom?

Q3 Draw a diagram of the atoms in a mixture of two different elements.

Q4 Six elements are shown on this page. Name six more elements.

2. Elements, compounds, mixtures

Compounds

Magnesium is an element. Let us see what happens to it when we burn it.

Q1 Copy this table.

	What colour is it?	Is it shiny?	Is it a powder?
Magnesium			
Burned magnesium			

Apparatus
- 5 cm piece of magnesium ribbon ■ Bunsen burner
- heat-proof mat ■ tongs

Safety note: Wear eye protection when burning magnesium. Do not look directly at the bright flame.

A Get a piece of magnesium from your teacher. Look at it carefully. Complete row **1** of your table.

B Use tongs to hold the magnesium in a Bunsen flame. Do not look directly at the bright flame.

C Look carefully at the burned magnesium and complete row **2** of your table.

When magnesium is burned, the atoms of magnesium join with atoms of oxygen from the air. This is a **chemical reaction**. The new material formed is **magnesium oxide**. It is a **compound**. It is completely different from both magnesium and oxygen.

A compound is a pure material which is made of two or more elements chemically joined together. A **molecule** is the smallest particle of a compound that can exist. It is made of two or more atoms joined together.

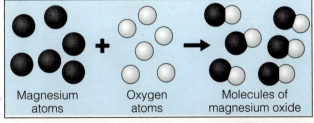

Magnesium atoms + Oxygen atoms → Molecules of magnesium oxide

Summary

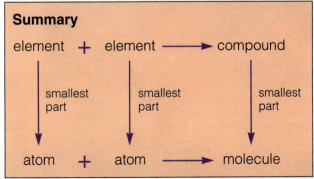

element + element → compound

smallest part ↓   smallest part ↓   smallest part ↓

atom + atom → molecule

Q2 Where did the oxygen come from in this experiment?

Q3 What is a compound?

Q4 What is a molecule?

Q5 Common salt is a compound. It is made from the elements **sodium** and **chlorine**. What do you think is the chemical name of common salt?

Extension exercise 1 can be used now.

2. Elements, compounds, mixtures

Mixtures

Most of the things around us are not pure materials. They are mixtures.

In a mixture materials are jumbled up together but they are not joined (**combined**) to each other.

A mixture can have different amounts of materials in it and still be a mixture. A sugar and water mixture is still a sugar and water mixture whether it has a little or a lot of sugar in it.

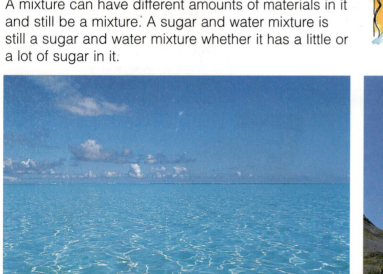

▲ At sea level air is a mixture of 78% **nitrogen**, 21% oxygen and 1% of other gases.

▲ At the top of a high mountain there is not much air. The air that is there only contains 20% oxygen.

▲ In the Dead Sea there is so much salt in the water that a person can float and cannot sink.

Q1 Explain in your own words what a mixture is.

Q2 Sort these materials into mixtures or pure materials: air, Coca-Cola, common salt, copper, oxygen, pizza, potato, seawater, tap water.

2. Elements, compounds, mixtures

Properties of mixtures and compounds

Remember that when elements combine they make a new material which is called a compound. A mixture is not a new material and it has the appearance and behaviour (**properties**) of the materials that are in it (its **constituents**).

Let us look at the elements **iron** and **sulphur** and at a mixture of them. We shall make them into a compound called **iron sulphide**.

Q1 Copy this table.

Name of material	What does it look like?	Is it magnetic?	Does it float or sink in water?
1 Iron			
2 Sulphur			
3 Iron/sulphur mixture			
4 Iron sulphide			

Apparatus

- iron filings ■ sulphur powder
- spatula ■ filter papers
- crucible ■ pipe-clay triangle
- tripod ■ Bunsen burner
- magnet ■ cling-film
- 100 cm³ beaker

Safety note: Wear eye protection at all times.

A Put one spatula of iron filings and one spatula of sulphur powder into a crucible. Mix them up well.

B Place the crucible on a pipe-clay triangle on a tripod in a fume cupboard. Heat the mixture strongly until it glows red.

C Leave the crucible to cool. Empty it on to a filter paper. This new material is a compound called iron sulphide.

D Put some iron filings on a second filter paper. Put some sulphur on a third filter paper. Make a mixture of iron and sulphur on a fourth filter paper. Look carefully at the four materials. Complete column **1** of your table.

E Cover a magnet in cling film. Hold the magnet just above each sample. Complete column **2** of your table.

F Use a spatula to put a small amount of each sample into water in a 100 cm³ beaker. Complete column **3** of your table.

Q2 Explain how a mixture of two elements is different to a compound made from the same two elements in:
a its properties
b the proportions of the two elements.

Extension exercises 2, 3, 4 and 5 can be used now.

3. Separating and purifying

Useful things from mixtures

Very few of the materials we use in our lives are found in nature as pure materials. They are almost always mixed with materials we do not want.

Scientists need to know how to separate the material they want from the other things in the mixture.

We get salt from the sea. The heat of the sun is used to **evaporate** the water.

All these useful articles are made from materials that can be separated from crude oil.

Some things are made of pure iron which is separated from iron ore (**haematite**).

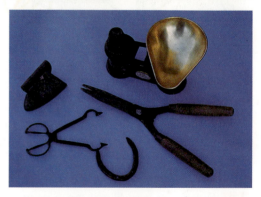

Q1 Oil, sea and trees are all natural materials. From which of them can we get: petrol, paper, plastic, rubber, salt?

Q2 Name two other natural materials and one material that can be got from each of them.

Extension exercise 6 can be used now.

3. Separating and purifying

Decanting

The simplest way of separating things is by **decanting**. This is used to separate a liquid and a solid that does not dissolve in it. You let the solid settle to the bottom and carefully pour the liquid into another container.

Apparatus
- 2 100 cm³ beakers
- 2 250 cm³ beakers
- spatula ■ salt ■ soil

Safety note: Wash your hands after handling soil.

A Get a 100 cm³ beaker and half fill it with water. Put four spatulas of soil into the water. Stir it well for one minute. Leave the mixture for five minutes.

B In another 100 cm³ beaker repeat step **A** using four spatulas of salt.

C Try to separate each of your mixtures by decanting into a 250 cm³ beaker.

Q1 Copy each of the following sentences. Write **'soluble'** (dissolves) or **'insoluble'** (does not dissolve) in each space:
   a Water will not decant away from salt because salt is _____ in water.
   b Water will decant away from soil because soil is _____ in water.

Q2 Copy the following sentence. Choose the correct word from the two in the brackets:
   Decanting is used to separate (soluble/insoluble) solids from (liquids/solids).

7

3. Separating and purifying

Filtering

Another way to separate a solid from a liquid is to sieve it. Scientists call this method **filtering**. Let's compare decanting and filtering.

Apparatus
- 100 cm³ beaker
- 2 conical flasks
- filter funnel
- filter paper
- spatula
- soil

A Half fill the beaker with water. Add four spatulas of soil. Stir it well. Leave it for one minute.

B Decant the water off into a conical flask. Put this to one side to look at later.

C Fold a filter paper to fit into a filter funnel (your teacher will show you how to do this if you have not done it before).
Put the filter funnel in the neck of a conical flask. Repeat **A** and pour the mixture through the filter paper.

D In **C** the water that comes through the filter paper is called the **filtrate**. Compare this filtrate with the decanted water from **B**.

Q1 Copy the sentences below. Use words from the list to fill in the blanks:

decanting liquid solid clearer filtrate

a Filtering is used to separate an insoluble _____ from a _____.

b The liquid obtained after filtering is called the _____.

c Filtering is a better method of separation than _____ because the liquid obtained is _____.

Q2 A spatula of salt is stirred in water.
Can you separate the salt and water by filtering? Explain your answer.

Extension exercise 7 can be used now.

3. Separating and purifying

Pure salt from rock salt

As we have seen, scientists often need to get pure materials from impure materials.

Let us see how our scientist can get pure salt from rock salt.

Apparatus

- rock salt ■ pestle and mortar
- $250\,cm^3$ beaker ■ spatula ■ filter funnel
- filter paper ■ conical flask ■ tripod
- evaporating dish ■ heat-proof mat
- gauze ■ Bunsen burner

Safety note:
Wear eye protection at all times!

Do not taste the solid left at the end!

Stop heating if the mixture begins to spit.

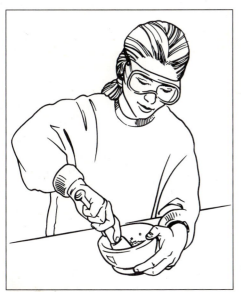

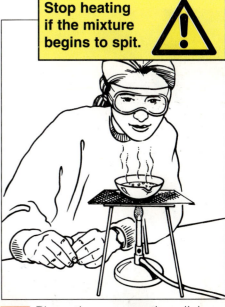

A Use a pestle and mortar to crush some rock salt into a fine powder.

B Use a spatula to put the crushed rock salt in the beaker. Half fill the beaker with water and stir thoroughly for a few minutes.

C Filter the mixture into a conical flask.

D Pour the filtrate into an evaporating dish. Do not fill the dish more than than two-thirds full.

E Place the evaporating dish on a tripod and gauze. Heat it with a Bunsen burner using a blue flame. As the water boils away turn the air-hole to half and turn the gas down a little. Turn off the Bunsen burner when the water has nearly gone.

Q1 Copy out sentences **a**, **b**, **c** and **d**. Use words from the list to fill in the blanks:
filtrate solution undissolved evaporated dissolves salt impurities residue filtration

a When crushed rock salt is added to water, the salt d_____ and forms salt s_____.

b The sand and other i_____ stay u_____.

c These are removed by f_____ and are called the r_____.

d The f_____ is e_____ to obtain pure s_____.

Extension exercise 8 can be used now.

3. Separating and purifying

Chromatography

Inks and dyes are mixtures of materials. Scientists often need to find out what is in them (**analyse** them). If a spot of ink is put in the middle of a filter paper and drops of water are put on it, the water spreads out and coloured rings are left on the filter paper.

The colours are the different materials in the ink. They separate out because they dissolve to a different extent in water.

▼ This process is called **chromatography**. It can be used in hospitals to help a hospital laboratory technician to find out which chemicals are present in a blood sample. This helps to tell whether a patient has an illness.

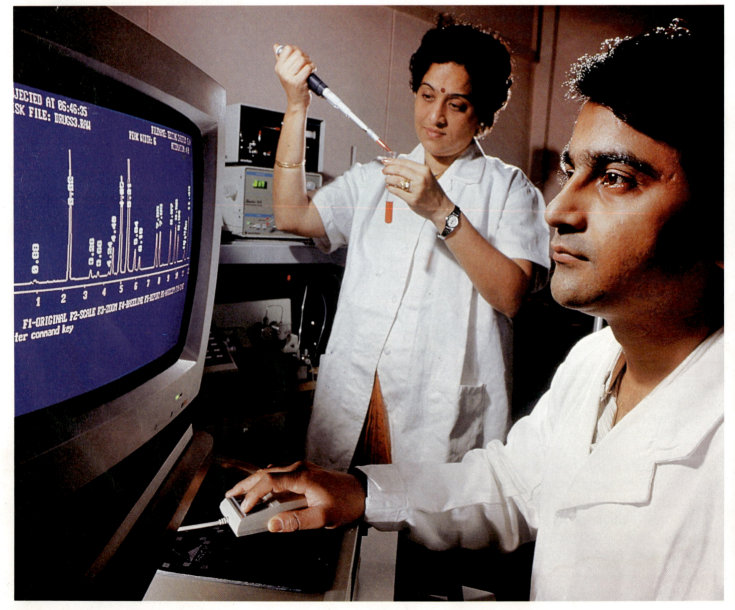

3. Separating and purifying

Apparatus
- dropper
- felt tip pens
- Petri dish
- filter paper
- paper towel

A Use a felt tip pen to make an ink dot about 3 mm in diameter in the middle of a filter paper.

B Put the filter paper on a Petri dish. Add one drop of water to the ink dot.

C When the drop has soaked in, add a second drop. Let this soak in. Continue adding drops until the water soaks to the edge of the filter paper.

D Leave the filter paper on a paper towel to dry.

E Repeat **A** to **D** with other colours of ink.

Q1 What is chromatography?

Q2 What is chromatography used for?

Extension exercise 9 can be used now.

4. Metals and non-metals

Metals

There are 92 natural elements.

We can divide these elements into metals and non-metals. About four-fifths (80%) of all the elements are metals. Many of them are rare and hard to find. Some common metals are very useful to us. You can see metals in use all around you.

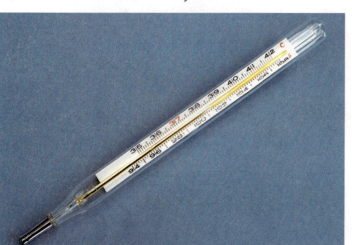

▲ Metals such as copper were used to make saucepans.

◀ Thermometers have mercury inside them. Mercury is the only metal which is liquid at room temperature.

▲ Iron can be mixed with other materials to make it stronger. These steel girders help to support buildings.

▲ Cars are made mainly of iron but other metals, such as chromium, zinc and copper, are used.

Q1 Name five metals.

Q2 What fraction of all the elements are non-metals?

Q3 State one use for each of the five metals you named in **Q1**.

4. Metals and non-metals

Non-metals

Only about one-fifth of the elements are non-metals but they are much more common and easier to find than metals.

At room temperature most non-metals are gases. Examples of these are hydrogen, oxygen, nitrogen. One non-metal, bromine, is a liquid (see photograph on page 2). A few, such as carbon and sulphur, are solid.

▲ Sulphur is a yellow solid. It can be obtained quite pure from inside the Earth.

▲ Purple iodine crystals can turn to a purple vapour without becoming liquid first.

▲ Green chlorine gas is used to purify the water in public swimming pools.

▲ The 'lead' in your pencil is not lead. It is carbon.

◀ Some non-metals, such as oxygen or nitrogen, are normally gases. They can be turned to liquid by high pressure and very low temperature.

Q1 Name five non-metals.

Q2 Name two elements which are liquid at room temperature.

Q3 What has to be done to air to make it turn to a liquid?

4. Metals and non-metals

Properties of metals and non-metals

In the picture you will see some words that can be used to describe the properties of a material.

Q1 Which of the properties in the cartoon do you think apply to metals?

Q2 Which of the properties in the cartoon do you think apply to non-metals?

4. Metals and non-metals

Classification

Metals have some properties which are the same as each other. For example, they are shiny.

Non-metals have some properties which are the same as each other. For example, solid non-metals will break easily (they are **brittle**). If you look at the properties of some elements you may be able to say whether they are metals or non-metals. Putting things into groups like this is called **classification**.

Apparatus
- samples of carbon, copper, iron, sulphur, zinc ■ spatula ■ tongs
- white tile ■ nail ■ fine emery paper
- 250 cm³ beaker

Q1 Copy this table.

Element	Appearance	Is it hard or soft?	Does it break or bend?	Is it shiny or dull?	Does it float in water?
Copper					

A Take a piece of copper foil. Note its appearance. Put it on the tile. Try to scratch it with the nail. Is it hard or soft?

B Hold the copper foil in two hands and try to break it or bend it.

C Hold the copper foil flat on the tile. Rub it gently with the emery paper to see if you can make it shine.

D Get a beaker. Half fill it with water. Put the copper foil into the water. Does it float or sink?

E Complete row 1 of your table.

F Repeat **A** to **D** for each of the other elements. Your teacher may demonstrate **A** to **D** with lead. Complete the whole of your table.

Q2 What are the properties of metals?

Q3 What are the properties of non-metals?

Q4 Elements can be classified as metals or non-metals. Describe two other ways of classifying elements.

Q5 A solid element X is heavy and not easy to scratch. Is it a non-metal or a metal?

Q6 A solid element Y can easily be bent into a shape and can be polished if rubbed hard. Is it a non-metal or a metal?

Extension exercise 10 can be used now.

5. Chemical reactions of metals

Reaction of metals with air

Metals are very important to us. Some metals go through chemical reactions which alter their properties. This can be inconvenient.

When a chemical attacks a metal we call it **corrosion**.

Air and rain are two substances which can cause metals to corrode.

A few metals do not corrode even when left exposed to air or weather for a long time.

▲ Things made from gold do not corrode even when left for thousands of years. This is thousands of years old.

▶ We have only recently begun to use some metals. Titanium does not corrode and can be used for things like replacement hip joints.

◀ Silver cutlery needs only to be lightly cleaned and rubbed every so often.

▲ We need to cook our food in saucepans that do not corrode. These stainless steel pans are excellent.

5. Chemical reactions of metals

Bridges and buildings can be made from metal. When the metal corrodes it causes many problems. Corroded metals have to be replaced.

▲ **Rusting** is the name given to the corrosion of iron. It costs the country millions of pounds every year.

▲ Metals are protected from corrosion by covering them up.

Paint can keep out air and rain. The painting has to be re-done regularly.

▶ Petroleum jelly is used to keep air away from battery terminals. It also keeps away acid that might leak from the battery.

Q1 Name two metals that are used to make jewellery. Explain why they are used.

Q2 Name three materials that can make a metal corrode.

Q3 Name two metals which corrode quite easily.

Q4 Describe two ways of preventing corrosion.

Q5 Why does corrosion cost the country millions of pounds each year?

5. Chemical reactions of metals

Reaction of metals with water

In this experiment magnesium and zinc are each put into cold water. Your teacher will demonstrate this experiment with calcium. Let's see if there are any differences between the metals or if there is any change if hot water is used instead of cold.

Adding metals to water

Q1 Copy this table.

Name of metal	What do you see when metal is added to cold water?	What do you see when metal is added to hot water?	Differences between using hot and cold water
Calcium Zinc Magnesium			

Apparatus

- 6 clean test tubes
- test tube rack
- 2 similar sized pieces each of magnesium and zinc ■ kettle
- labels ■ tweezers

Safety note: Wear eye protection at all times.

A Get three test tubes. Label them A, B and C. Put about 3 cm depth of cold water into each of them.

B Use tweezers. With care, quickly put a piece of zinc into tube A, and a piece of magnesium into tube B.

C Watch the test tubes carefully for about three minutes. Compare them with the control C.

D Complete column **1** of your table.

5. Chemical reactions of metals

E Boil some water in the kettle. Repeat **A**, **B** and **C** using hot water instead of cold water.

F Complete columns **2** and **3** of your table.

Q2 How do you know when a chemical reaction is taking place in the test tubes?

Q3 In cold water, which metal reacted the fastest?

Q4 In cold water, which metal reacted the slowest?

Q5 In hot water, which metal reacted the fastest?

Q6 In hot water, which metal reacted the slowest?

Q7 Describe any difference the hot water made.

Extension exercise 11 can be used now.

5. Chemical reactions of metals

Heating metals in air

When an element burns in air it joins with oxygen to form an **oxide**.

Let us see what happens when some metals are heated in air.

Q1 Copy this table.

Name of metal	Appearance of metal before heating	Appearance after heating	Did change happen slowly, quickly, not at all?
Copper			

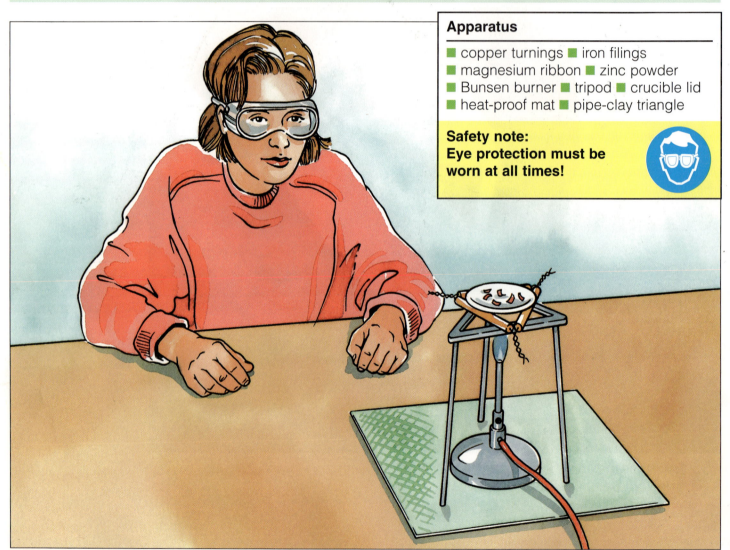

Apparatus
- copper turnings ■ iron filings
- magnesium ribbon ■ zinc powder
- Bunsen burner ■ tripod ■ crucible lid
- heat-proof mat ■ pipe-clay triangle

Safety note: Eye protection must be worn at all times!

A Put some copper turnings on a crucible lid. Put the lid on a pipe-clay triangle on a tripod. Heat it strongly for at least five minutes. Complete row **1** of your table.

B Repeat **A** for iron filings, magnesium ribbon and zinc powder. Complete the rest of your table. Your teacher may demonstrate what happens when lead foil is heated in air.

Q2 Write a list of the metals used in order of how easily they reacted. Start with the most reactive.

Q3 Explain the difference between 'burning' something and 'heating' something.

5. Chemical reactions of metals

Putting metals into acid

Let us see what happens when the metals are put into acid.

Apparatus
- copper turnings ■ clean iron nail
- magnesium ribbon ■ metal tongs
- granulated zinc ■ 5 test tubes
- rubber bung to fit test tubes
- test-tube rack ■ wooden spill
- dilute hydrochloric acid
- eye protection

Safety note: Eye protection must be worn at all times!

Q1 Copy this table.

Name of metal	Do bubbles appear?	Do the bubbles appear quickly or slowly?	Did the spill 'pop'?
Magnesium			

A Take a test tube. Put it in a test-tube rack. Put about 3 cm depth of dilute hydrochloric acid into it. Add a piece of magnesium ribbon.

B Leave the test tube to stand for about five minutes or until bubbles appear. If bubbles appear a gas is being made. Put a bung loosely in the test tube for about 10 seconds to let the gas build up.

C Remove the bung and quickly hold a lighted spill at the mouth of the test tube. If the gas burns with a 'pop' then it is hydrogen. Complete row **1** of your table.

D Repeat **A** to **C** with each of the other metals you have been given. Your teacher may demonstrate **A** to **C** using lead foil. Complete the table.

Q2 Write a list of the metals in the order of how quickly bubbles were produced. Put the quickest first.

Q3 Name one metal which reacts with air and with acid.

Q4 Name a metal that does not react with acid.

Q5 If you wear a gold ring when washing up, will the ring be harmed? Explain your answer.

Q6 Why is it a bad idea to make bracelets out of magnesium?

6. Word equations

All chemical reactions can be represented by a word equation.

This is much shorter than writing whole sentences but it still tells us what has happened.

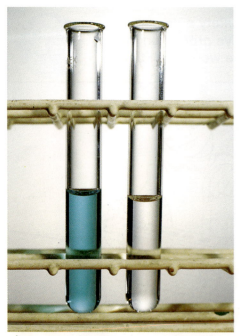

▲ Here we see blue copper sulphate solution in one test-tube and colourless sodium hydroxide solution in another. They are going to be put together to make a **chemical reaction**. They are called the **reactants**.

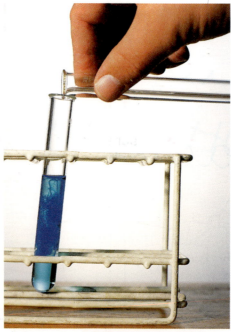

▲ The copper sulphate solution and the sodium hydroxide solution are mixed together. A chemical reaction takes place.

▲ The mixture produced is filtered. There is a light-blue solid in the filter paper. This solid is called copper hydroxide. There is also a colourless solution in the test tube called sodium sulphate. These are the **products**.

You can see that we have used three paragraphs of words to explain what happened in the reaction.

This explanation can also be written in the form of a word equation.

| copper sulphate + sodium hydroxide ⟶ copper hydroxide + sodium sulphate |

You can also use the word equation to describe the appearance of the reactants and the products.

| copper sulphate + sodium hydroxide ⟶ copper hydroxide + sodium sulphate |
| (blue solution) (colourless solution) (light-blue solid) (colourless solution) |

6. Word equations

Let's look at some of the reactions you have already done and write word equations for them.

▶ On page 3 there is an experiment in which you burned magnesium ribbon in air. In this experiment the reactants are magnesium and oxygen and the product is magnesium oxide.

The chemical word equation for this reaction is:

> magnesium + oxygen ⟶ magnesium oxide

A descriptive chemical word equation is:

> magnesium + oxygen ⟶ magnesium oxide
> (metallic ribbon) (gas from air) (white powder)

▶ On page 21 you did an experiment in which you added zinc to hydrochloric acid.

In this experiment, the reactants are zinc and hydrochloric acid. The products are hydrogen (the gas that bubbles out) and zinc chloride (the solution left in the test tube).

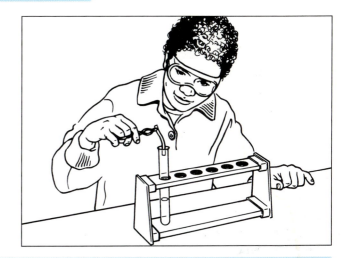

The word equation is:

> zinc + hydrochloric acid ⟶ zinc chloride + hydrogen

A descriptive chemical word equation is:

> zinc + hydrochloric acid ⟶ zinc chloride + hydrogen
> (metallic pieces) (dilute, colourless solution) (colourless solution) (colourless gas)

Q1 What is meant by 'reactants'?

Q2 What is meant by 'products'?

Q3 When pieces of calcium are added to water, bubbles of hydrogen are seen and calcium hydroxide solution is left.
 a Which substances are the reactants?
 b Which substances are the products?
 c Write a word equation for the reaction.

Extension exercise 12 can be used now.

7. Comparing the reactivity of metals

We have seen that metals have similar properties.
They differ in how fast they make chemical reactions.

▲ Some metals react so quickly that they are dangerous.

▲ Some metals react so slowly that they do not seem to react at all.

Looking back at the experiments you have done with metals will enable you to write a list of metals in order of how fast they react. This list is called the **reactivity series**. It is a kind of league table that puts the most reactive metals at the top.

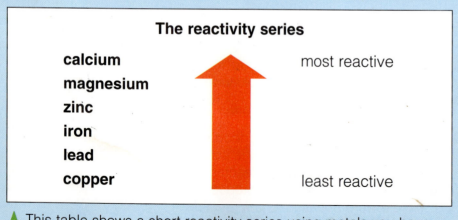

▲ This table shows a short reactivity series using metals you have worked with in this book.

Q1 Write down the following metals in order of reactivity. Put the most reactive first:

lead magnesium calcium iron copper zinc.

Q2 Name a metal that is more reactive than zinc.

Q3 Name two metals that are less reactive than zinc.

Q4 Putting potassium into acid would cause a reaction that is extremely dangerous. Where would you place potassium in your reactivity series? Explain your answer.